Wings

by Helen Gregory

Consultant:
Adria F. Klein, Ph.D.
California State University, San Bernardino

capstone
classroom

Heinemann Raintree • Red Brick Learning
division of Capstone

Many animals have wings. Some animals use their wings to fly.

This bird spreads its wings to fly.

Bird wings have feathers to help them fly.

Wings can be colorful.
Wings keep a bird warm.

Insects have wings, too.

Bees have wings.

Butterfly wings have many colors.

This moth has large spots to scare away enemies.

Ladybugs hide their wings under hard shells.

Grasshoppers use their wings to make sounds.

Only one mammal has wings. It is the bat.

Penguins have wings but cannot fly. They use their wings to swim.

Some animals have wings but cannot fly or swim.

An ostrich cannot fly.
It is too heavy.

This swan's wings
are beautiful!